HORSE BONDS: YOUR JOURNEY TO TRUST AND UNDERSTANDING

AN INTERACTIVE BOOK WITH 41 KEY INSIGHTS FOR DEEPENING HORSEMANSHIP, EQUINE THERAPY, AND PERSONAL GROWTH

MARCEL OLIVÉ

www.marcelolive.com

Working with horses involves inherent risks, and each horse is unique in its temperament and behaviour. Therefore, the author, publisher, and any contributors to this book cannot be held responsible for any accidents, injuries, or damages that may result from the application of the ideas, techniques, or suggestions contained herein. It is essential that readers exercise caution, seek professional guidance, and assess their horse's individual needs. By reading this book, you acknowledge the importance of taking responsibility for your actions, using your own judgment and prioritising the well-being of both yourself and your horse.

ISBN: 9798340356765

CONTENTS

INTRODUCTION

Welcome to this journey of understanding and connecting with horses. Through years of research, reading, learning, courses, certificates, experimenting, experiencing, training, feeling, and growing alongside horses and humans, I have acquired principles and practices that have transformed my approach to horsemanship. I have learned that the bond between a human and a horse is one of the most profound connections that can be cultivated. My philosophy centres on respect, empathy, and mutual understanding. I believe in a gentle approach to training that honours the horse's natural behaviours and instincts, fostering a relationship built on trust and cooperation.

Are you looking to deepen your connection with your horse? Or perhaps you are seeking ways to enhance your horsemanship skills? Even looking for a kit of transformational tools for your work in equine therapy, facilitation, learning, or coaching? These unique horsemanship key insights, designed as a tool to achieve just that, are based on a collection of quotes, each paired with reflective questions and interactive insights. They offer a valuable self-learning experience for both novice and experienced equine practitioners, providing effective and transformational insights that can be applied directly to horses. Use them to inspire thoughtful discussions, self-assessment, and continuous growth in your journey with your horse.

These insights cover a comprehensive range of essential themes such as respect and patience, calmness and presence, trust and partnership, effective communication, positive training, adaptability and problem-solving, and enjoyment and playfulness. Each theme is not just a standalone concept but a part of a comprehensive approach to horsemanship. This holistic design ensures that you are addressing all aspects of your relationship with your horse, offering a strong, respectful, and joyful foundation for your journey.

Additionally, these insights are not just for personal horsemanship. They are a fantastic toolbox for equine-assisted learning, coaching, or therapy. Discussing horsemanship and horse behaviours using these interactive insights is an excellent method to influence, support, inspire, self-reflect, and learn about human behaviour. Horses act as mirrors to our emotions and actions, making them powerful facilitators for personal growth and self-awareness. By observing and interacting with horses, individuals can gain insights into their own behaviour patterns, emotional responses, and communication styles. This reflective process, facilitated by the horsemanship insights, fosters a deeper understanding of oneself and others, promoting empathy, emotional regulation, and effective communication.

At the heart of horsemanship lies the profound relationship between humans and horses. This bond is not just a nice-to-have but a crucial element in achieving your training goals. It should be built on mutual respect, trust, and communication. A strong human-horse relationship enhances the effectiveness of training and contributes to the overall well-being of both horse and rider. It is through understanding and empathy that we can create a harmonious partnership where the horse feels safe, valued, and willing to cooperate. This connection is not only essential for achieving training goals but also for ensuring that the horse leads a happy, healthy life. By investing time and effort into building this relationship, we lay the groundwork for a fulfilling and rewarding experience for both horse and handler.

Trust is the foundation of a successful human/horse relationship. Building trust involves consistent, respectful interactions where the horse feels safe and valued. Gentle handling and patience help develop a bond where the horse is willing to cooperate and engage.

Empathy is crucial in understanding and responding to a horse's needs and emotions. By seeing the world from the horse's perspective, we can create a more compassionate and effective training environment. Empathy involves listening to the horse's signals and responding with kindness and understanding, fostering a deeper connection.

Patience and consistency are vital in horsemanship. Horses learn at their own pace, and rushing the process can lead to stress and resistance. Consistent cues and routines help horses understand what is expected of them, building confidence and security. Patience allows for gradual progress, ensuring that the horse feels comfortable and supported throughout the training journey.

By integrating these principles into your approach, you can create a harmonious and rewarding partnership with your horse, where both of you grow and learn together. The purpose of these insights is to help you and your community achieve a true connection with your horse – a partnership where achievement and performance are attained through flowing together, making fulfilment your ultimate reward. Start your journey with this book and transform your relationship with your horse today.

HOW TO USE THIS BOOK WITH 41 INTERACTIVE INSIGHTS FOR DEEPENING HORSEMANSHIP, EQUINE THERAPY, AND PERSONAL GROWTH

This book is designed to enrich your experience and deepen your understanding of horsemanship. There are many ways you can integrate its insights into your daily practices to enhance your relationship with your horse.

Here's how to make the most out of them:

- Familiarize yourself with the themes. Each insight belongs to one of the following themes: Respect and Patience, Calmness and Presence, Trust and Partnership, Effective Communication, Positive Training, Adaptability and Problem Solving, and Enjoyment and Playfulness. Understanding these themes is crucial as they represent the core principles of successful horsemanship and will guide your interactions with your horse.

- One approach is to use these insights for daily reflection. Select one each day or week to reflect on. Read the quote and consider the reflective questions and interactive insights provided on the back of the page. Spend a few moments thinking about how this principle applies to your current training and relationship with a horse.

- Incorporate the selected insight into your training sessions. Bring it to your training sessions and use it as a focal point for that session. For example, if the insight emphasises patience, consciously practice being more patient and observe how your horse responds. Reflect on your experience after the session and note any changes or improvements.

- These insights are also excellent tools for group discussions and workshops. Share one with your group and facilitate a discussion around the quote and questions. Encourage participants to share their experiences and insights, too. This collaborative approach can lead to deeper understanding and shared learning.

- For those involved in equine-assisted learning, coaching, or therapy, these insights are incredibly valuable. Use them to guide sessions, helping clients reflect on their behaviours, emotions, and interactions with the horse. Horses act as mirrors to our inner states, and this book can help facilitate meaningful conversations and personal growth.

Each insight comes with open-ended questions that encourage reflection not only about equine interactions but also about human behaviour. For example, the question "How do you show respect to your horse every day?" can be expanded to include "How do we show respect to people?" Similarly, the question "How do you think your mood and attitude affect your horse during training?" can be extended to ask, "How do you think your mood and attitude affect the people around you?"

Using these insights, you can create thought-provoking and engaging discussions that encourage clients to draw parallels between their interactions with horses and people. This approach helps promote self-awareness, empathy, and personal development, making these insights a powerful tool in equine-assisted settings.

- Another effective method is to keep a journal to document your reflections and progress. Write down the quote, your thoughts on the reflective questions, and any observations from your training sessions. Over time, this journal will become a valuable record of your journey and growth in horsemanship.

- If you are a trainer or educator, these insights can enhance your teaching methods. Use them to introduce key concepts and foster discussions among your students. This content can also serve as a starting point for practical exercises, helping students apply theoretical knowledge in real-world situations.

- Based on the insights' theme and questions, you can develop custom exercises tailored to your horse's needs. For instance, if focusing on "Trust and Partnership", you might develop exercises that build trust through gentle handling and consistent cues. Customising exercises ensures that the training is relevant and beneficial for both you and your horse.

- Use this book to practice mindfulness and presence with your horse. Before starting your session, read an insight and set an intention based on its message. This practice helps centre your mind, fostering a calm, focused interaction with your horse.

- Periodically review the insights you have used and reflect on your progress. Assess how these principles have influenced your horsemanship skills and your relationship with your horse. Regular reflection helps reinforce learning and highlights areas for continued growth.

By integrating these insights into your daily routine, training sessions, and reflective practices, you will not only enhance your skills but also deepen the bond with your horse. This book is designed to be a continuous source of inspiration and guidance, helping you and your horse achieve a harmonious and fulfilling partnership. Enjoy the journey!

RESPECT AND PATIENCE

"The key is not asking the horse to respect you. The key is you respecting the horse, then they will be open to you"

Marcel Olivé

The key is not asking the horse to respect you. The key is you respecting the horse, then they will be open to you.

- How do you show respect to your horse every day?
- Can you remember a time when respecting your horse's comfort led to something good happening?
- What signs do horses give you to show they are comfortable or uncomfortable?

Respect is the foundation of all good relationships, including those with horses. Many people think that the horse must respect us first. But in reality, we need to respect the horse first. This approach helps us build a stronger, more understanding bond.

Respect does not mean making a horse do what we want, expecting their compliance. It means seeing horses as living beings with their own needs, feelings, and limits. It's not just about being kind; it's about understanding and being patient. It is to think about the horse's happiness in everything we do, from grooming to training.

Watching and listening are very important in respecting a horse. By paying close attention to what a horse likes, dislikes, and fears, we can change our behaviour to better suit the horse. This helps us create routines and training methods that make the horse feel safe and comfortable.

> " No violence is a must, as is training without anger. Do not be mad; smile, and have fun.

Marcel Olivé "

No violence is a must, as is training without anger. Do not be mad; smile, and have fun.

- How do you think your mood and attitude affect your horse during training?
- Can you share a time when staying calm and positive led to a good training session?
- What are some ways you stay patient and happy while working with your horse?

Respecting the principle of non-violence and training without anger is key to having a good relationship with your horse. Horses can sense your feelings. When you are calm and happy, your horse will feel that way, too. Your horse might become tense and uncooperative if you are angry and frustrated.

Keeping a positive attitude and having fun during training makes it enjoyable for both you and your horse. Smiling and having a good time can make training a happy experience. This helps your horse learn with positive feelings, making them more willing to engage and learn.

By being patient, kind, and joyful, you create a safe and caring environment for your horse. This not only helps with learning but also builds trust and respect. The goal is to train your horse and have a lasting, positive relationship based on understanding and kindness.

> " Have patience to be patient so you do not need patience with your horse.

Marcel Olivé

Have patience to be patient so you do not need patience with your horse.

- How do you find patience in yourself during training sessions?
- Can you remember a time when being patient with your horse helped them learn something new?
- What are some ways to remind yourself to stay calm and patient when things get tough?

Patience is very important for horse trainers. It's not just something you do, but a way of being. When we have real patience, we do not just try to be patient; it becomes a natural part of how we work with our horses. This kind of patience helps us handle problems with understanding and kindness. It shows that being patient changes how we train, making it a normal part of how we treat our horses.

In horse training, "slow is faster" shows why patience is so important. Taking things slowly and calmly reduces stress and helps horses learn better. This training approach builds a stronger bond between horse and trainer. Trust and understanding are developed by noticing and respecting a horse's feelings and capabilities, turning challenges into opportunities for growth.

When patience becomes a part of who we are, not just a trick we use, we handle training with more care and kindness. This approach puts the horse's needs first and helps create a happy and successful partnership. Being mindful and patient makes the training journey as enjoyable and fulfilling as reaching our goals.

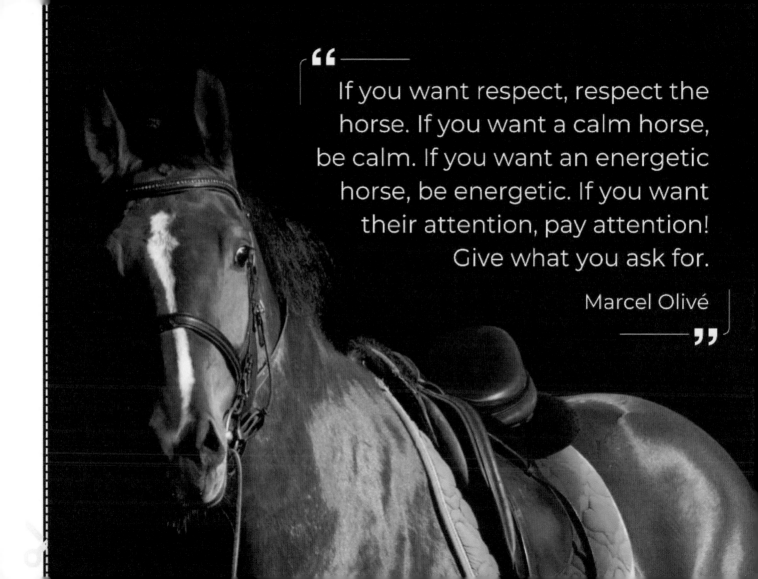

> "If you want respect, respect the horse. If you want a calm horse, be calm. If you want an energetic horse, be energetic. If you want their attention, pay attention! Give what you ask for.
>
> Marcel Olivé"

If you want respect, respect the horse. If you want a calm horse, be calm. If you want an energetic horse, be energetic. If you want their attention, pay attention! Give what you ask for.

- How do your emotions and behaviour influence your horse's responses during training?
- Can you share an experience where your calmness or energy directly impacted your horse's behaviour?
- What strategies do you use to maintain the qualities you want to see in your horse?

This principle is a powerful reminder of the influence we have as horse trainers. It emphasizes leading by example in horse training. Horses mirror the behaviour and emotions of their handlers, making it essential to embody the qualities you wish to see in your horse. This is not just a responsibility but an opportunity to inspire and motivate your horse to be the best it can be.

Respecting the horse involves handling it with kindness, patience, and understanding, fostering mutual respect and cooperation. Maintaining a calm demeanour helps keep the horse calm, reducing stress and enhancing focus. Conversely, exuding energy and enthusiasm can encourage the horse to be more responsive and engaged.

This approach underscores the importance of self-awareness and emotional regulation in training. You create a harmonious and effective training environment by reflecting your desired behaviour in your horse. Ultimately, leading by example improves the horse's behaviour and strengthens the bond between horse and handler, making training sessions more productive and enjoyable.

> Acknowledgement creates engagement, engagement creates connection, and connection creates friendship. Acknowledge your horse.
>
> Marcel Olivé

Acknowledgement creates engagement, engagement creates connection, and connection creates friendship. Acknowledge your horse.

- How do you notice and respond when your horse tries to talk to you?
- Can you tell about a time when listening to your horse's signals made something good happen?
- What are some ways you can become closer friends with your horse?

Building a strong, lasting relationship with your horse starts with noticing how they try to talk to you. Acknowledging your horse is the first step to forming a deep bond. It shows you are aware of your horse's efforts to communicate. By recognising your horse's signals, you show that you value their attempts to interact. Responding to these signals, whether by a simple nod, a gentle touch, or a friendly word, tells your horse that you are listening and paying attention.

When you notice your horse's efforts, you naturally start to involve them more. This means inviting your horse to join in activities and decisions, encouraging them to take part and feel important. As you keep recognising and involving your horse, a deep connection forms. This connection is built on trust and understanding, where you and your horse work together happily. Your horse becomes more eager to follow your directions and join in activities, knowing they are part of a team.

Eventually, this journey leads to a real friendship with your horse. Friendship comes from always recognising and involving your horse and building a relationship based on respect and happiness. This friendship makes every moment with your horse special, turning each time together into a shared adventure of understanding and companionship.

> **You are what you do. What do you do to the horse?**
> Marcel Olivé

You are what you do. What do you do to the horse?

- How do your actions and behaviour affect your horse's feelings and responses?
- Can you share a time when being kind and patient with your horse made a big difference?
- How do you want to be seen, and what do you need to do to make it possible with your horse?

Building a strong friendship with your horse starts with how you treat the horse. Horses are very good at understanding your feelings and actions. When you are kind, patient, and gentle, you show your horse that you care about them and respect their feelings. This helps build trust and makes your horse more willing to follow and work with you.

Think about how you want your horse to see you. Do you want to be a kind and trusted friend? If so, you need to act in a way that shows your horse you are someone they can rely on. Being gentle and patient creates a place where your horse feels safe and happy.

Remember, your actions show who you are, not just to your horse but to everyone around you. By being a good friend to your horse, you show them that you are someone they can trust. This creates a friendship based on respect and kindness, making your time together more fun and enjoyable.

CALMNESS AND PRESENCE

CALMNESS AND PRESENCE

Breathe, breathe, and breathe all day long - that is what I do with horses.

Marcel Olivé

Breathe, breathe and breathe all day long – that is what I do with horses.

- How does your breathing affect your horse when you train together?
- Can you remember a time when breathing calmly helped make a stressful situation with your horse better?
- What are some ways you use breathing to stay calm and focused when you train with your horse?

Breathing deeply and focusing on your breath is very important in horse training. It helps both you and your horse feel safe and calm by keeping stress levels low.

Breathing is not just about taking in air; it also helps control emotions. When you breathe deeply and stay calm, your horse can feel it and become calmer. When you let out a deep breath, it tells your horse that everything is okay and there's nothing to worry about.

Starting your training sessions with deep, soft breaths sets a peaceful mood. If something stressful happens, stopping to breathe calmly can help keep things from getting more tense. When you take a break, a soft breath can make your horse relax and lower its head, showing trust and connection.

Breathing calmly on purpose keeps stress levels low, helps to stop the fight-or-flight reaction, and creates a better training environment.

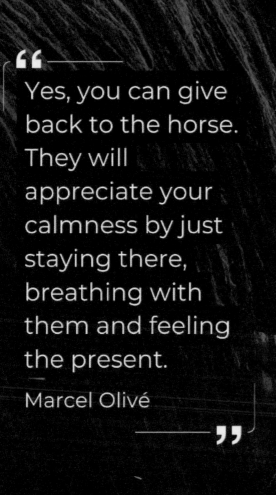

> " Yes, you can give back to the horse. They will appreciate your calmness by just staying there, breathing with them and feeling the present.
>
> Marcel Olivé
> "

Yes, you can give back to the horse. They will appreciate your calmness by just staying there, breathing with them and feeling the present.

- How do you practice being fully present with your horse?
- Can you recall a moment when your calm presence positively impacted your horse?
- What are some ways you can give back to your horse?

In horse care, it is easy to overlook the small but important ways we can give back to our horses. Besides just feeding and training them, horses also value our presence and the quiet moments we share. Simple actions like staying calm, breathing together, and being fully present can create a strong bond.

A calm presence makes horses feel safe. When we stay relaxed and gentle, it helps them feel peaceful, especially when they are nervous. Breathing together with your horse can also make a big difference. Matching our breaths with theirs creates a deep connection and helps both of us feel calm.

Being fully present means focusing on your horse without any distractions. This could be during grooming, riding, or just standing together. When we give our full attention to our horses, they feel respected and valued. These quiet, focused moments build trust and strengthen our relationship with them.

Follow the path of softness with your horse by being non-judgemental and calm, and you will achieve softness in all your actions.

Marcel Olivé

Follow the path of softness with your horse by being non-judgemental and calm, and you will achieve softness in all your actions.

- How can you be non-judgmental and calm in your interactions with your horse?
- Can you share an experience where a calm and non-judgmental approach led to a positive outcome with your horse?
- What strategies can you use to maintain a soft approach in challenging situations?

Softness in horse care is more than just a technique – it is an approach that includes emotional and psychological aspects. To embrace softness, start by having a non-judgmental mindset. Put aside any preconceived ideas and see each horse's behaviour as a result of their instincts, experiences, or discomforts. This encourages empathy.

Patience and observation are important. Approach situations without making negative judgments. Learn how your horse communicates to build a deeper bond, which helps you understand and respond to their needs better. Keeping calm is also crucial. Horses react to the emotions around them. Staying serene reassures your horse, making them feel safe and calm. Consistent, calm behaviour helps build a dependable relationship.

Softness goes beyond physical touch – it is about your intentions. Gentle handling that prioritises the horse's comfort and responds to their feedback fosters trust. In training and riding, use minimal pressure and clear, gentle cues. Work together with the horse, guiding them with patience. Being responsive rather than reactive makes the horse feel acknowledged and valued. This practice not only improves training but also strengthens the bond, making every moment a step towards a deeper mutual understanding.

> "If you feel you have to do something to help the horse, but you do not know what, then just do nothing or go for a walk with your horse."
>
> Marcel Olivé

If you feel you have to do something to help the horse, but you do not know what, then just do nothing or go for a walk with your horse.

- Have you ever found peace in just spending quiet time with your horse?
- Can you share a moment when a simple walk or quiet time with your horse was especially rewarding?
- How do you incorporate unstructured time into your routine with your horse?

In a busy world, we often overlook the simple joys of bonding with our horses. Not every moment with them needs a specific purpose; sometimes, the best connections come from just being together. Taking a leisurely walk or sharing quiet moments allows your relationship to grow naturally.

When you have some spare time or need a break, remember that meaningful interactions with your horse do not always need elaborate plans. Simple activities, like taking a stroll or just sitting quietly together, can strengthen your bond. These moments help you find peace and contentment while nurturing your relationship.

Embracing simplicity helps you and your horse connect on a deeper level. Quiet time together can be profoundly satisfying, fostering a sense of appreciation for each other's presence. Just sitting and observing your horse can teach you a lot about their natural behaviours and personality. Walking beside your horse encourages mindfulness, helping you notice small details.

This quiet companionship time can be a source of healing and comfort, especially during stressful times. Even without a goal, spending time with your horse enriches your relationship and strengthens your bond. Embracing simplicity allows for a natural and profound connection.

Being mad with a horse is like being mad with yourself. It's useless and does not help anyone.

Marcel Olivé

Being mad with a horse is like being mad with yourself. It's useless and does not help anyone.

- How do you stay calm and patient when your horse does not understand something?
- Can you think of a time when staying positive helped you and your horse have fun?
- What can you do to make training with your horse a pleasant experience for both of you?

Horses can sense how we feel, just like we can tell when someone is happy or upset. When we get mad at a horse, it does not help either of us because the horse might get confused or scared.

Think about how you feel when someone is mad at you. It does not feel nice, right? It's the same for horses. They might not know what they did wrong. Instead of getting angry, take a deep breath and try to understand what might be bothering them.

Horses learn best when we are kind and patient with them. When things do not go as planned, try to stay calm and think about how you can help your horse understand what you want. Sometimes, it helps break things down into smaller steps that are easier for them to learn.

Having fun with your horse makes training a lot more enjoyable! You can try new activities that your horse likes, give them plenty of encouragement, and praise them when they do well. Remember, training with your horse is about teamwork. When you stay positive and calm, your horse will feel it, and both of you will have a great time learning and growing together.

TRUST AND PARTNERSHIP

TRUST AND PARTNERSHIP

"Trust is earned. Gain the horses' trust and trust them; you will gain a willing partner.

Marcel Olivé "

Trust is earned. Gain the horses' trust and trust them; you will gain a willing partner.

- How do you build trust with your horse every day?
- Can you share a time when trust was very important between you and your horse?
- How can you make sure you act the same way each day to help your horse trust you?

Trust is earned by showing care, patience, and understanding. It starts with the first time you meet your horse and grows over time. It is very important to make sure your horse feels safe and respected. Being consistent is key. Horses like it when things are predictable. When you act the same way each day, your horse learns that they can rely on you. This makes them feel more comfortable and trusting.

Trust also means respecting and listening to your horse. Just as you want your horse to trust you, you need to trust your horse, too. Pay close attention to their signals and what they are trying to tell you. This mutual trust is the foundation of a strong partnership.

Patience is really important for building trust. Every horse learns at their own speed. Respecting this helps keep trust strong. Celebrate the small steps your horse makes. This creates a happy and trusting environment.

A horse that trusts you will be happy to work with you. This comes from positive experiences and mutual respect. It is important to notice early signs if your horse is having trust issues. By nurturing trust and keeping communication clear, you can deepen your bond and improve the well-being of both you and your horse.

"
The horse
should not do
things for you.
You should do
things together.

Marcel Olivé
"

The horse should not do things for you. You should do things together.

- How do you incorporate the idea of partnership into your training with your horse?
- Can you share an experience where working together with your horse led to a positive outcome?
- What changes can you make to ensure you and your horse are working as a team?

This message means we should see our relationships with horses as partnerships instead of thinking we should always be in charge. It is about working together and showing respect to each other instead of just telling the horse what to do all the time. Remember, your horse is not just a tool for your work but a partner who deserves your respect.

Instead of thinking of horses as animals we control, this new way of thinking suggests that we should treat them as our friends and teammates. Horses are not just followers; they are active members of our team.

Being partners with horses means we have to understand and respect what they can do, how they feel, and what they need. We need to see horses as living creatures with their own likes and dislikes, and it's important that we ask for their consent, too.

This partnership means we need to communicate with our horses both ways, paying close attention to their body language and how they respond to us. By doing this, we can build a stronger friendship and have better training sessions that make both us and the horses happy.

"

Show who is the horse's... friend!

Marcel Olivé

"

Show who is the horse's... friend!

- How can you show your horse that you are their friend?
- Can you share a moment where empathy and understanding improved your relationship with your horse?
- What actions can you take to build a partnership based on friendship with your horse?

Equine care should move away from dominance-based methods to relationships built on friendship and mutual respect. This correct approach emphasises understanding, companionship, and empathy, recognising horses as beings with their own personalities and emotions.

Training can become playful and fun, making learning enjoyable and less stressful. This makes the horse more eager to participate and deepens the bond between you. Moments of quiet companionship, like walking or grazing together, help strengthen your relationship and allow both of you to relax and connect deeply.

Horses treated with consistent kindness respond with affection and trust. Redefining leadership as a partnership based on friendship shows that you do not need to be dominant to guide effectively. This approach nurtures a bond founded on empathy, respect, and shared positive experiences, enriching the lives of both the horse and the handler.

> "We help horses to be with humans when we train horses."
>
> Marcel Olivé

We help horses to be with humans when we train horses.

- How do you help your horse adapt to life with humans when you train the horse?
- Can you share an experience where the horse reacted as you trained and made a difference in your horse's life?
- What are some ways you ensure your training methods respect the horse's nature?

When we train horses, we help them adapt to life with humans. Horses have to learn everything we ask of them because it is all unnatural to them. They do not need us, but we seek their companionship and help. Training horses does not make them dependent on us; it helps them live with us. Each cue and lesson is like teaching a new language. Horses live by instincts refined over thousands of years, yet we expect them to adapt to our world.

We are not just teaching them skills for our benefit; we are helping them adjust to life with us. This requires respect, understanding, and patience. Horses do not naturally carry riders, pull carriages, or perform in arenas. They have to learn every step, turn, and stop under our command and cues.

In training, we act as translators and guides, bridging their world and ours. We ask them to trust, understand, and adapt. In return, we must offer safety, companionship, purpose, and a commitment to their well-being. They enrich our lives, and in training, we should honour their trust, celebrate their intelligence, and blend their spirits into our world.

"
The greater the freedom, the deeper the connection. Connection is based on freedom of choice.

Marcel Olivé

"

The greater the freedom, the deeper the connection. Connection is based on freedom of choice.

- How does letting your horse have more freedom change your relationship with them?
- Can you share a time when allowing your horse to make a choice made your bond stronger?
- What are some ways you can let your horse make choices during training?

Letting horses have freedom when they are with us helps us build a stronger and more real connection. When horses can make choices, they become partners with us rather than just followers. This freedom helps them trust us more and feel respected because they know we value them.

When horses are free to choose, training becomes teamwork. Instead of making them always follow orders, we create a space where they want to join in. This shows we respect their intelligence and allows them to feel confident and in control.

The key to a strong bond with your horse is letting them have the freedom to choose. This freedom helps build trust and respect and makes the relationship more meaningful. By valuing their choices, we create a partnership based on understanding and a real connection.

"
Make a deal
with your horse
and spread
responsibilities.
Remember
that we are
looking for a
real
partnership.

Marcel Olivé

"

Make a deal with your horse and spread responsibilities. Remember that we are looking for a real partnership.

- How can you share responsibilities with your horse to build a stronger partnership?
- Can you describe a time when letting your horse make decisions made your time together better?
- What are some ways you can show your horse you appreciate what they do?

In horsemanship, making a deal with your horse means working together as partners. Sharing responsibilities and decisions helps you and your horse build a strong bond.

Giving your horse responsibilities does not mean giving up control but letting the horse make some choices. Horses are smart and can make good decisions. For example, when you go on a ride, you can choose where to go, while your horse can decide where to step and alert you if there are any dangers. You build trust and cooperation by listening to your horse and giving feedback.

This way of working creates a friendly relationship based on respect. Communication becomes more detailed, with the horse understanding your cues and you noticing their signals. Riding and working with your horse becomes more fun when you both appreciate each other's help.

Sharing responsibilities makes your partnership stronger. Decide what your horse is good at and praise them when they do it well. Working together like this helps both of you grow and improves your connection.

EFFECTIVE COMMUNICATION

> It is all about communication. It is foolish to insist if the horse does not understand you. Make sure they know what you are asking.
>
> Marcel Olivé

It is all about communication. It is foolish to insist if the horse does not understand you. Make sure they know what you are asking.

- How do you make sure you and your horse understand each other during training?
- Can you remember a time when you and your horse misunderstood each other? How did you fix it?
- How do you help your horse understand your signals and commands?

The key to having a good relationship with horses is being able to talk to them clearly. Asking a horse to do something they do not understand does not help and can make them lose trust in you. It is important that horses understand our signals and commands so they can learn and work with us happily.

Talking to horses is not just about telling them what to do but also about listening to what they are saying. If a horse does not do what you ask, it means you might need to change how you ask. This ensures your horse knows what you want in a way they can understand.

To cue clearly with your horse, you must be patient and do things the same way each time. It is also important to learn how horses behave and think. By using signals your horse knows, being kind, and having a gentle approach, you can help your horse feel safe and respected. When they understand you, horses are more excited to learn and work with you.

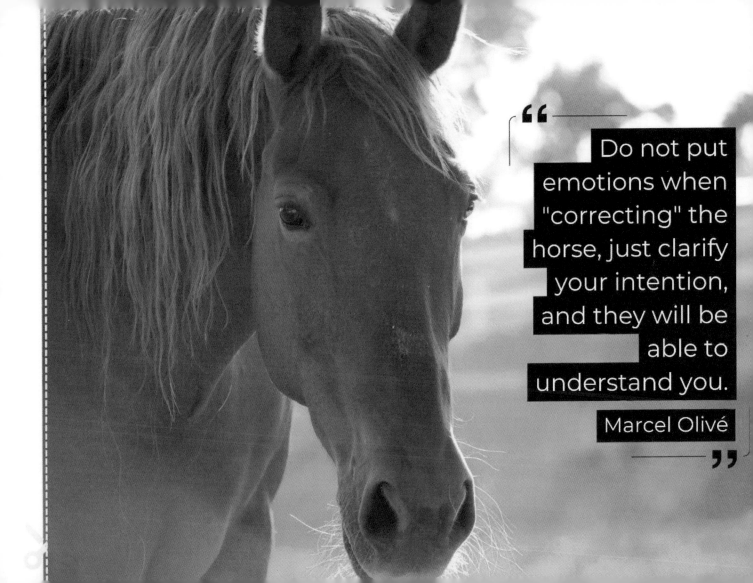

> Do not put emotions when "correcting" the horse, just clarify your intention, and they will be able to understand you.
>
> Marcel Olivé

Do not put emotions when "correcting" the horse, just clarify your intention, and they will be able to understand you.

- How do you make sure your instructions to your horse are clear and kind, without anger?
- Can you tell about a time when being calm helped your horse understand better?
- How can you keep yourself calm and clear when teaching your horse?

When you are training your horse, it is important to communicate clearly and stay calm. This means giving clear instructions and corrections without getting upset. Horses need to understand what you want from them, so it is best to be precise and consistent.

How you feel can really affect how well your horse learns. Horses can sense our emotions, so they are more likely to listen and learn if we stay patient and positive. This means that keeping a calm attitude is very important for successful training.

Good training is more than just teaching tricks. It is about building a friendship with your horse. When you are clear and calm, your horse feels safe and respected, and this makes them eager to work with you. Remember, training is not just about teaching your horse new things; it is about growing and understanding each other better every day.

> "Attention, purpose, intention, cue... and the horse will do it.
>
> Marcel Olivé

Attention, purpose, intention, cue... and the horse will do it.

- How can you ensure you pay full attention to your horse when you are together?
- Can you think of a time when knowing exactly what you wanted to do helped your horse perform better?
- What are some easy ways you use to show your horse what you want them to do?

In horse performance, the way you pay attention, have a purpose, set your intention, and give cues is very important for successful communication with your horse. Each of these steps helps guide your horse and makes communication clear and smooth.

Start every interaction by giving your full attention to your horse. Be present and watch how your horse is feeling. This shows your horse that you are paying attention, making them more likely to cooperate because they feel noticed and understood. Have a clear purpose for what you are doing with your horse, whether it is training or just going for a walk. Make sure your actions show this purpose so your horse understands what is expected. Turn your purpose into intention by planning in your mind what you want your horse to do. Communicate your intention consistently through your body language and cues. Give your cues gently but clearly. Make sure they are easy for your horse to understand, and do not confuse them. Recognise when your horse responds correctly to help them learn.

When you pay attention, have a clear purpose, set intentions, and give cues all at once, your horse is more likely to do what you want. This shows a relationship built on trust, respect, and good communication.

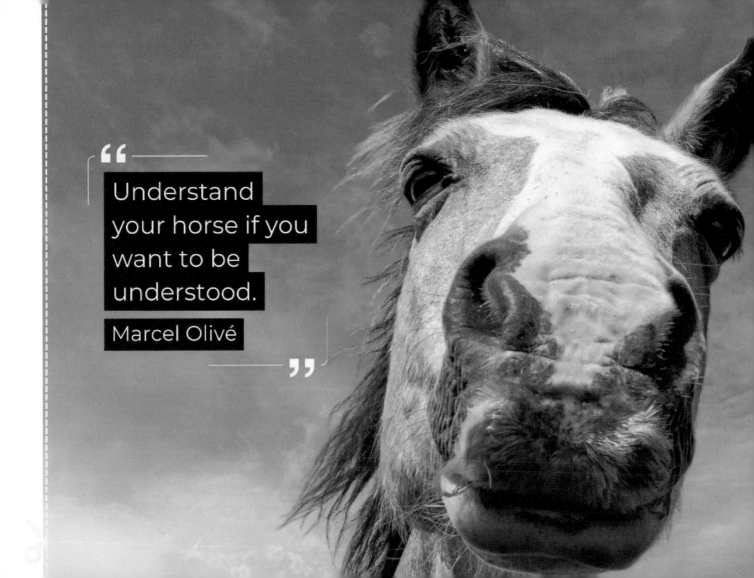

> **Understand your horse if you want to be understood.**
>
> Marcel Olivé

Understand your horse if you want to be understood.

- How do you notice and react to the signals your horse gives you?
- Can you tell about a time when understanding your horse's behaviour helped you get along better?
- What can you do to learn more about how your horse communicates in its own special way?

Learning to understand and communicate with horses in their own way helps people and horses get along better and build strong friendships.

Look out for signs like fear, anxiety, comfort, and playfulness to understand how your horse feels. When you see these signs, respond to them so your horse knows you are listening. This helps build trust and makes your bond stronger. Try not to misunderstand what your horse is saying, as this can make things tricky. Focus on building real friendships with your horse.

Talking to your horse is not about being the boss but about respect, listening, and understanding. Horses are great at reading body language, so watch how you stand and move. Gentle touches can show your horse you care. Soft strokes on their neck or withers can be comforting, and speaking calmly helps keep things relaxed.

Watch for signals from your horse's ears, eyes, head, tail, and body. Learn what their movements mean. By understanding how horses move and behave, we can communicate better. This mutual understanding is key to building trust and respect, which is essential for a great friendship with your horse.

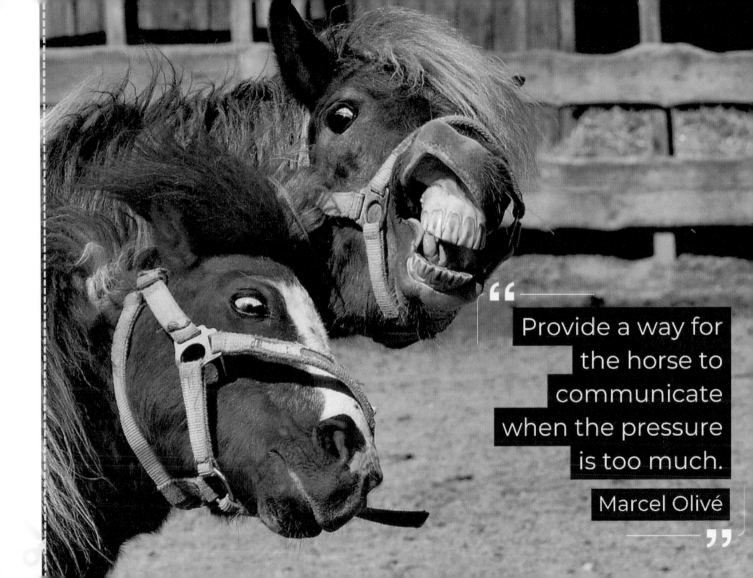

Provide a way for the horse to communicate when the pressure is too much.

Marcel Olivé

Provide a way for the horse to communicate when the pressure is too much.

- How do you let your horse show you when they feel too much pressure?
- Can you describe a time when noticing that you were applying too much pressure helped you to rectify and improve your training session?
- What are some ways you can include this approach in your daily routine with your horse?

The principle of allowing a horse to communicate when pressure is too much might seem counterintuitive. Traditional training often emphasises the human as the boss. However, true leadership and respect are built on mutual understanding and the ability to listen. For instance, teaching an uncatchable horse by empowering them to influence your actions can be transformative. Simple cues, such as "If you look at me with both eyes, I'll retreat," shift the dynamic, incorporating empathy and consent into the training process.

Understanding the horse's perspective is essential. Horses, as prey animals, perceive pressure as a potential threat. By giving them a way to signal discomfort, we honour their instinctual need for safety. This requires patience and awareness of the horse's body language.

The goal is to foster a partnership based on trust and respect. Allowing a horse to communicate its comfort level with pressure leads to a deeper, more empathetic relationship, enhancing training outcomes and the overall bond between horse and handler.

If you want connection, always answer your horse when they tell you something.

Marcel Olivé

If you want connection, always answer your horse when they tell you something.

- How do you notice and respond to your horse's cues?
- Can you share a time when understanding your horse's signals made your bond stronger?
- What do you do to make sure you and your horse understand each other well?

Effective communication with a horse extends beyond words; it is a nuanced dance of mutual understanding. True understanding and being understood are vital for a strong bond in equine care and training.

Building a meaningful connection requires consistently acknowledging and responding to the horse's cues and behaviours, ensuring the horse feels heard and valued. To comprehend a horse, observe their non-verbal language: body language, ear positioning, eye expressions, and tail movements. Vocalisations like whinnies or snorts also provide insights.

Humans must be clear with consistent cues, body signals, voice commands, and positive training; projecting calm and assertive energy helps make communications effective.

Responding to a horse's communication is essential. Acknowledge and adapt to their signals to build trust. Modify training methods or change the approach to interactions as needed. Each response strengthens the bond, making each interaction a building block in a relationship of mutual respect.

POSITIVE TRAINING

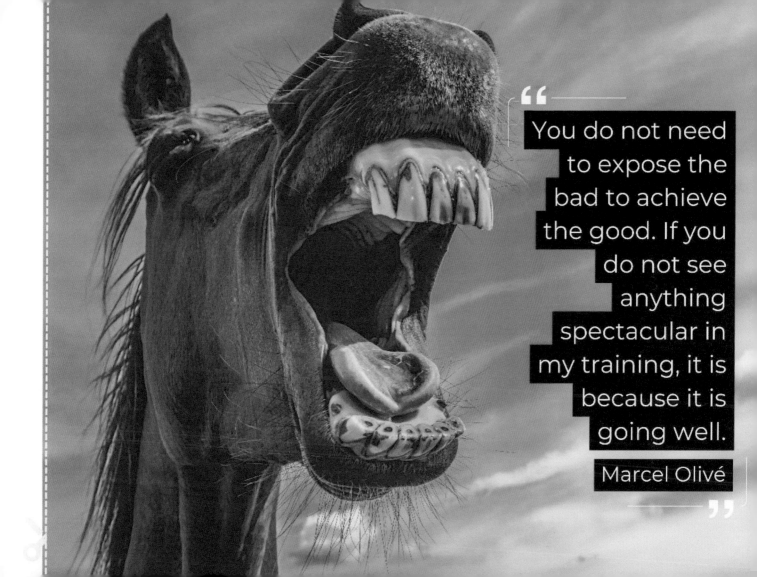

"You do not need to expose the bad to achieve the good. If you do not see anything spectacular in my training, it is because it is going well.

Marcel Olivé

You do not need to expose the bad to achieve the good. If you do not see anything spectacular in my training, it is because it is going well.

- How do you stop problems from getting worse during your training sessions?
- Can you remember a time when small progress showed that your training was working well?
- What are some things you do to keep your horse calm and avoid big reactions?

Good training means solving problems before they happen. This means creating a positive and supportive environment where the horse can feel safe and comfortable. By rewarding good behaviour and creating positive experiences, you can help stop bad behaviour from happening in the first place. This makes training more fun and less stressful for your horse and you.

Many people think you need to trigger and see bad behaviour to correct it, but that is not always true. You do not need to wait for a horse to do something wrong to fix it. Good training does not have to involve drama. In fact, a calm and smooth session often means that the training is going well. If your horse seems more willing, focused, or relaxed, it shows you are making progress.

Understanding your horse's needs and helping them before they become problems is kinder and more effective. If a horse feels like they might fail or get into trouble, they can become stressed and anxious. When a horse trusts you, they will be more willing to listen and learn. Over time, your horse will learn and grow from positive experiences, not because they are scared of getting something wrong.

"Always focus on the good rather than on the wrong. Ask yourself, what was good about what the horse just gave me?

Marcel Olivé

Always focus on the good rather than on the wrong. Ask yourself, what was good about what the horse just gave me?

- How do you think about mistakes during your training sessions?
- Can you tell about a time when looking at the good things your horse did help the horse get better at something?
- How can you find something good in what your horse did, even if there was a mistake?

In horse training, mistakes are not problems; they are chances to learn and grow. When horses make mistakes, it is important to see what went well and what can be learned. Each mistake can help us improve how we train and talk to our horses.

Understanding that mistakes are part of learning helps us change our approach when needed. Mistakes give us clues about what needs more work or if we should resume it from another angle. This way, horses can try new things without worrying about getting into trouble, which helps them become more confident.

It is important to celebrate small improvements. When you notice and praise these little steps forward, it encourages your horse to keep getting better. Focusing on what your horse does right makes them feel relaxed and happy to learn, creating a positive and supportive training environment for both of you.

> If you want high performance with your horse, then, less correction and more connection!
>
> Marcel Olivé

If you want high performance with your horse, then, less correction and more connection!

- How do you make sure you balance correction and connection when you are training?
- Can you share a time when focusing on connection helped your horse perform better?
- What things do you do to build a stronger bond with your horse?

Switching from focusing on correcting mistakes to building deeper connections with your horse can lead to better results. Traditional training often relies on correction, but this can damage trust and make the horse perform out of fear. Instead, aim to understand your horse better, which helps them perform willingly and accurately.

Too much correction can make your horse feel forced to do things, hurting the bond between you. Correction should be gentle and paired with positive rewards. A strong connection is built on trust and respect, achieved through consistent communication and fair treatment.

Connection is key to good performance. A deep understanding between you and your horse is essential for success. This bond allows both of you to communicate effectively and trust each other completely. Building an emotional bond requires spending quality time together and creating a positive atmosphere. Clear communication and consistent cues are crucial to forming a strong connection.

A horse that feels truly connected is more focused and flexible, which is important for high performance. By focusing on connection instead of correction, you can improve your horse's performance and well-being.

> "Believe in the process and just flow without skipping any step.
>
> Marcel Olivé "

Believe in the process and just flow without skipping any step.

- How do you stay confident in your training?
- Can you think of a time when trusting your training helped you and your horse achieve something special?
- What do you do to keep motivated when training gets tough?

Believing in how you train your horse is really important if you want to reach your big goals. Being sure of what you are doing and trusting that your horse can learn are key, even when it feels like things are moving slowly. Imagine what success looks like, and remember that every little step takes you closer to where you want to be.

Things will not always go perfectly, but if you keep trying and stick to a good training process, you will see progress over time. It is also important to be flexible and understand what your horse needs as it learns. Every step you complete gets you closer to your big goal.

Just because something is hard does not mean you have failed – it might just mean you need to spend a bit more time on it. Think about what you have done well in the past to help you feel more confident, and ask experienced trainers for help if you need it. Celebrate small victories to see how far you have come.

Believing in your training plan helps your horse feel calm and happy. Horses like it when their trainers are confident and calm, which helps them trust you and learn better. Believing in what you are doing ensures that you can achieve your goals.

"Do not cross thresholds if you want to raise them.

Marcel Olivé

Do not cross thresholds if you want to raise them.

- How can you tell when your horse is close to their limit?
- Can you tell about a time when listening to your horse's limits made your training better?
- What do you do to slowly help your horse handle more challenges?

In horse training, thresholds are like limits that show when a horse starts feeling uncomfortable or cannot handle something. Knowing where these limits are and respecting them is important for building trust and making sure training goes well. Things like past experiences and personality affect a horse's thresholds. You can tell when a horse is near their limit by watching for signs like a tense body, trying to move away, a faster heartbeat, or even small things like flicking ears or swishing their tail.

If you push a horse past their limit, it can get stressed or scared, and it might stop trusting you. Going past these limits too often can make the horse anxious or not want to cooperate. Respecting the horse's limits helps make a good learning space. If you help a horse face new things slowly, step by step, they stay calm and learn better. This approach builds a strong bond with the horse based on respect and understanding, helping the horse become stronger and more adaptable.

When you introduce new things to your horse, do it in small, easy steps. Pay attention to how the horse reacts so you know when to keep going or when to pause and let the horse adjust. Managing these limits well means noticing when the horse is uncomfortable and helping them feel better.

By respecting your horse's limits, you make learning positive, help the horse feel good, and strengthen your connection. This will make your horse more confident, stronger, and eager to learn.

"The horse's curiosity is a gift for the trainer. So, use it because it is a gift for you.

Marcel Olivé

The horse's curiosity is a gift for the trainer. So, use it because it is a gift for you.

- How do you make your horse interested and curious when you are training together?
- Can you tell a story about a time when letting your horse be curious helped them learn something new?
- What are some fun activities you can try to make your horse more curious and excited to learn?

Encouraging your horse's natural curiosity helps you and your horse grow closer together. You can create fun experiences where both of you explore and learn new things. For example, you can take your horse for walks in new places or introduce safe objects for them to investigate during training.

Let your horse sniff, paw, and explore different objects. Join in and interact with these objects together with your horse. You can turn training into a playful adventure by setting up a fun obstacle course. This makes learning exciting for your horse. When you explore together, it shows your horse that new experiences with you are safe and fun. This strengthens your bond and helps your horse trust your leadership.

These activities are good for your horse's mind and body, and they also help your horse feel less anxious about new situations. Regularly engaging your horse in these stimulating activities makes them more eager and attentive during training sessions. Encouraging your horse's curiosity enriches their environment and builds a stronger friendship between you and your horse. By creating positive experiences with new things, you help your horse become a confident and adaptable partner.

ADAPTABILITY AND PROBLEM SOLVING

> "If it is not working, go back one step in your lesson and continue incrementally."
>
> Marcel Olivé

If it is not working, go back one step in your lesson and continue incrementally.

- How do you know when it is time to take a break from training your horse?
- Can you share a time when going back to basics helped solve a problem with your horse?
- What are some ways you make sure your horse remembers the basic skills during training?

Running into problems is part of training horses. When something is not working, it is often best to go back to basics. This means practising simpler skills to help your horse feel more confident and less frustrated. Remember, patience is key. Sometimes, a horse struggles because it needs more practice with a basic skill.

Do not be afraid to practise the basics again. A strong foundation is important for learning harder skills. Start by seeing where your horse feels happy and confident, then adjust your training plan to fit. Break down difficult tasks into smaller steps, making them easier if needed.

Once your horse has mastered the basics, you can slowly add more challenging tasks. Every horse learns at its own speed, so make sure you move at a pace that works for your horse. Celebrate each small achievement to boost your horse's confidence and eagerness to learn.

Going back to basics helps you and your horse understand each other better, building a stronger bond. While this approach may seem slower, it usually leads to better, longer-lasting learning. Taking a step back is a smart way to ensure that every step forward is taken with confidence and clarity.

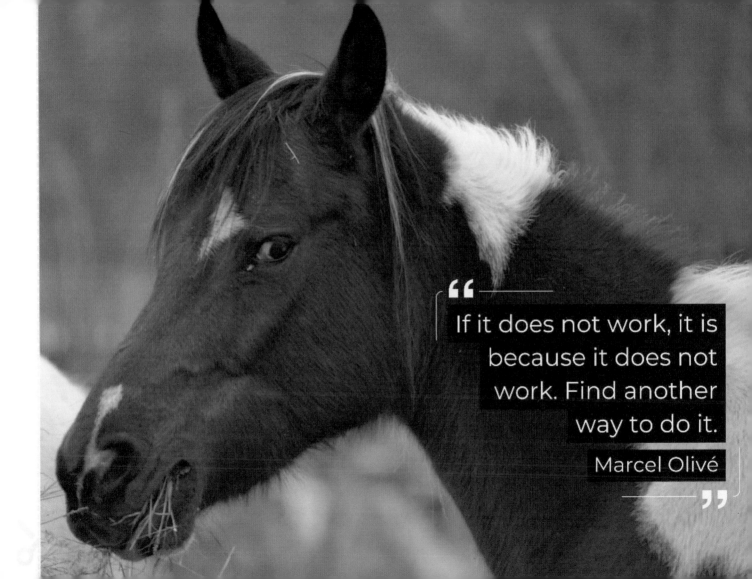

> " If it does not work, it is because it does not work. Find another way to do it.

Marcel Olivé

"

If it does not work, it is because it does not work. Find another way to do it.

- How do you know when a training method is not working?
- Can you share a time when changing how you trained helped you succeed?
- What are some ways you stay flexible and creative while training your horse?

This message emphasises flexibility and adaptability in horse training. Not all horses respond the same way, so trainers must adjust methods to suit each horse's needs. Persistence in a failing strategy does not benefit the horse or the trainer. It is crucial to reevaluate and adjust your approach if a strategy fails. Often, failure is due to unclear communication, impatience, rushing, or incorrect processes. Sticking to ineffective methods wastes time and stresses the horse, affecting learning.

When facing resistance, stepping back and considering alternatives is beneficial. Observation is key: identify what is not working by looking for signs of stress or discomfort. Reflect on the process and identify potential causes for the lack of progress. Flexibility and creativity are crucial for finding new solutions.

Adapting training methods involves breaking tasks into smaller steps, using positive training, or adjusting the environment. This trial-and-error process requires continuous learning and adaptation. Prioritising the horse's well-being builds trust and cooperation, leading to more effective training outcomes. Horses respond positively to methods that respect their individuality and limits. This approach fosters a positive and productive relationship, ensuring better results and a more harmonious bond between horse and trainer.

> **Each mistake is a step forward in the lesson.**
>
> Marcel Olivé

Each mistake is a step forward in the lesson.

- How do you think about mistakes when you train your horse?
- Can you tell about a time when looking at the good side of things helped your horse do better?
- What do you do to help your horse to have a better learning experience?

Seeing mistakes as opportunities to learn can improve training. Mistakes are just wrong answers to questions we ask. For example, if you ask your horse to move forward and the horse shakes their head, it is like your horse is trying to talk to you, not ignoring you. The horse might be confused or uncomfortable, so it is important to listen and figure out what is happening.

Mistakes give you important information about what needs more work. When you think of mistakes as part of learning, you can change how you train to help your horse understand better. Appreciate these tries instead of seeing them as failures. This makes a safe space for your horse to learn. Building confidence is really important. When horses know they will not get into trouble for mistakes, they are happier to try again. Focus on what your horse does right.

Think about why a mistake happened and learn from it. Ask yourself, "What good thing my horse just gave me?" Celebrate the small wins. Noticing little steps forward helps your horse behave well and want to keep improving. Keep adjusting based on what you learn from mistakes to improve your training.

When you focus on what is good, your horse feels relaxed, listens better, and wants to learn more. This way of training makes things positive and fun for both you and your horse.

> And release... You have thought what just has happened.
>
> Marcel Olivé

And release... You have thought what just has happened.

- How do you make sure you stop putting pressure on your horse at the right time during training?
- Can you share a time when letting go of pressure at the right moment made your horse learn better?
- What are the potential effects of rewarding a horse following bad behaviour?

This message shows why it is important to think carefully and act quickly when training horses. When we put pressure on a horse, it is not to make them uncomfortable but to guide them to do what we teach. The key is to release the pressure as soon as the horse does the right thing. This tells the horse has done well and acts like a reward.

For the horse, the release of pressure is a strong signal. It learns that doing the right thing makes the pressure go away, which feels good. Over time, the horse understands that listening to us makes things more comfortable.

It is important to consider when you let go of the pressure. For example, if you gently pull down on the lead rope and the horse lifts the head, letting go at that moment teaches the horse that lifting the head stops the pressure. But if you want the horse to lower their head, keep gentle pressure until the horse starts to lower the head. Then, let go to show the horse that lowering the head is what you want.

After each training session, think about what just has happened and how your actions affected the horse's response. This helps ensure that when you let go of the pressure, you teach the horse the right thing. Without thinking about it, you might accidentally teach the horse to do the wrong things.

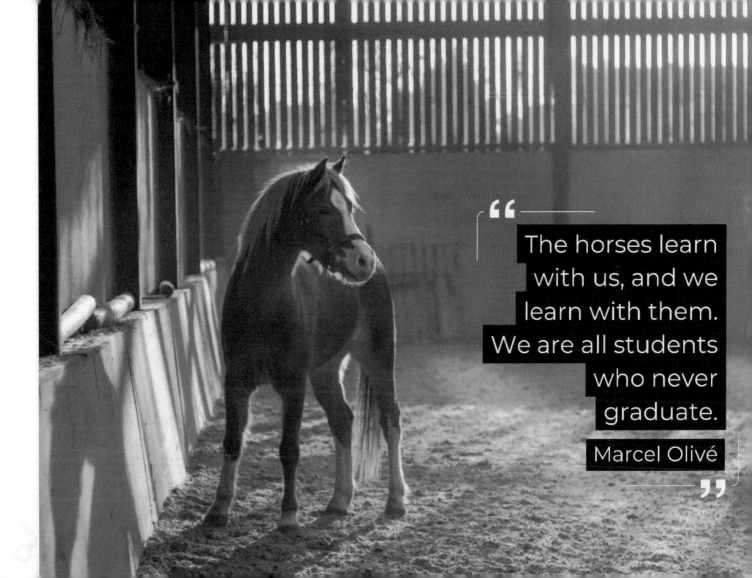

> The horses learn with us, and we learn with them. We are all students who never graduate.
>
> Marcel Olivé

The horses learn with us, and we learn with them. We are all students who never graduate.

- How do you learn from your horse during training?
- Can you share a time when both you and your horse learned something new together?
- What does it mean to you that training is about learning together?

In horse training, both horses and humans are always learning together. Humans learn about patience, empathy, communication, and horse behaviour. Horses, which are clever animals and not machines, also teach us a lot as they learn. They can learn everything from basic ground manners to complicated riding techniques. For example, a horse stops not because we keep pulling on the bit in its mouth but because the horse has learned that stopping makes the pressure go away. When humans interact with horses, it is always a shared learning experience for both.

Good training requires clear communication and understanding to create a willing partnership. Training is all about simplicity, patience, and understanding. Overcomplicating things can lead to unnecessary miscommunication. Spending time training correctly builds a strong connection, making it rewarding for both you and your horse.

Training should be kind, focusing on mutual respect. We must reward desired behaviours and avoid mixed signals that confuse horses. Training is a two-way process that offers us insights into how horses see the world. Through empathy, patience, and understanding, we build a relationship that enriches both horses and humans.

"Not all horses are the same. Learn to recognise their differences.

Marcel Olivé

Not all horses are the same. Learn to recognise their differences.

- How can you tell when a horse is different from others and how they react and communicate?
- Can you share a time when recognising your horse's unique traits helped your training or friendship?
- What are some ways you can adapt to your horse's differences?

Just like people, each horse is special and has its own personality. Some horses are bold and confident, while others might be a bit shy and need more time to get used to things. Paying attention to how your horse acts and communicates can help you understand what they need and how they feel.

It is also important to see how your horse behaves with other horses. Some horses make friends easily and love spending time with their buddies. Keeping horse friends together can make them feel relaxed and happy.

When you notice your horse is having trouble with something, try breaking it down into smaller steps they can handle. This can make learning new things easier for them.

Understanding what makes your horse unique can show them respect and kindness. This helps build a trusting friendship where your horse feels loved and understood. Appreciating what makes each horse special improves how you care for them and makes spending time with them a fun and rewarding experience.

ENJOYMENT AND PLAYFULNESS

ENJOYMENT AND PLAYFULNESS

"'Love' is in the air. Air, hair, skin, muscle. You should aim for the air.

Marcel Olivé

"Love" is in the air. Air, hair, skin, muscle. You should aim for the air.

- How do you practice using the lightest touch in your training?
- Can you share an example where a minimal cue was effective?
- What does it mean to you to aim for the "air" in your interactions with your horse?

The philosophy of "Air, hair, skin, muscle" in horse training highlights the importance of starting with the gentlest touch possible, like a soft whisper of air, and only increasing contact if necessary. This approach focuses on communicating with the horse using subtle cues and only applying more pressure if the horse does not respond. When the horse responds correctly, the pressure is released at that level, reinforcing the desired behaviour.

This method respects the horse's sensitivity and intelligence, fostering understanding and compliance through gentle cues. The key is that our softness allows us to determine if a light cue, like a skin touch, is enough, avoiding unnecessary pressure. If the horse responds to these minimal cues, there is no need to increase physical interaction.

This approach cultivates a harmonious relationship based on mutual respect and subtle communication. It encourages trainers to be mindful and gentle, enhancing the horse's responsiveness and trust. By aiming for the "air," we honour the horse's natural sensitivity and promote a training environment rooted in patience and empathy.

Just flow - freedom is flowing.

Marcel Olivé

Just flow – freedom is flowing.

- How do you create a sense of flow with your horse during training?
- Can you share an experience where you and your horse were perfectly in sync?
- What steps do you take to ensure adaptability in your interactions with your horse?

The concept of 'flow' in horse training is about moving in harmony with your horse, creating smooth and natural interactions. True freedom with your horse is achieved when you both move together naturally. Flow frees you from strict expectations and the need to force results. It allows you to take what is happening now and guide it toward your goal, like riding a wave.

Embracing flow means being adaptable and responding to your horse's needs and actions. Horses live in the present, and by matching this mindset, you create a harmonious partnership. Instead of forcing strict expectations, you move with the horse, adjusting and guiding to build trust and understanding. Flow is finding a rhythm with your horse that feels easy and natural, creating a dance of shared understanding. It means letting go of the need to control everything about your horse's behaviour and focusing on guiding and responding intuitively.

Being in flow means being responsive instead of reactive, understanding and predicting your horse's needs and movements. This state allows both you and your horse to let go of tension and stress, offering a sense of emotional freedom.

When you achieve this state of flow, training sessions become a smooth dance of communication and cooperation, turning routine tasks into moments of connection and shared joy. This deepens the bond between you and your horse, creating a partnership built on mutual respect and harmony.

> " It is your attitude and mindfulness that will make you have fun with your horse.
>
> Marcel Olivé "

It is your attitude and mindfulness that will make you have fun with your horse.

- What is mindfulness, and why can it enhance your time with your horse?
- Can you share a moment when being fully present with your horse created a memorable experience?
- What are some ways you practice connection and positivity during your interactions with your horse?

The true joy of spending time with your horse lies in your approach. Mindfulness – being fully present and engaged – transforms everyday interactions into moments of joy and connection. Be present and fully immerse yourself in each experience, whether grooming, riding, or simply spending time together. Engage with the sights, sounds, and sensations around you, focusing on the interaction. Notice how your horse moves, their coat's texture, and their breathing rhythm.

Approach each activity feeling your senses. Cherish your horse's unique qualities and the special moments you share. Express appreciation for your horse's efforts, patience, and companionship, creating a positive environment. Maintain a positive attitude, even during challenges. See obstacles as opportunities to learn and grow with your horse. Embrace setbacks as part of the journey and keep an optimistic outlook.

Be mindful of your emotions and their impact on your horse. Horses are highly sensitive to human emotions, and a calm, positive demeanour can greatly enhance the experience for both of you. If you are feeling frustrated or anxious, take a moment to breathe and centre yourself before continuing. Your horse will appreciate your calmness and respond better to your cues.

Let's Play! Embrace the joy of togetherness.

Marcel Olivé

Let's Play! Embrace the joy of togetherness.

- How do you incorporate play into your routine with your horse?
- Can you share a memorable moment of play with your horse?
- What benefits have you noticed from adding playfulness to your interactions?

Playing with your horse makes you both happy and helps you become better friends. Adding play to your time together makes things fun and exciting. It helps your horse learn and lets them be curious. Play allows your horse to act naturally like they would with other horses. It gives them something interesting to think about and helps you both trust each other more.

Turn lessons into games, making learning fun and less stressful for your horse. You can also let your horse move around freely in a safe area while you just watch (*if you are in the arena, always use a helmet and keep a safe distance to avoid sudden movements or kicks*). Spending time exploring new places together helps you and your horse discover interesting things along the way. Even training can become playful if you approach it with this playful mindset.

When you play, just enjoy being with your horse. Notice how your horse reacts and change what you do if needed. Every horse is different, so enjoy their special ways.

Playing is good for your horse's body and mind and makes them happy. These fun times help you build a strong friendship. Playing is not just about training but enjoying each other's company. Let's play and enjoy our journey with our horses!

And... smile!

Marcel Olivé

And... smile!

- How do your feelings and facial expressions change how your horse acts?
- Can you remember a time when being happy and cheerful helped you and your horse get along better?
- How can you include more positive actions, like smiling, when you are with your horse every day?

Smiling is important when you are with horses because they can see and react to our faces. When you smile, it creates a happy mood and changes how you and your horse feel and act.

When you smile, your body releases chemicals called endorphins that make you feel happier and less stressed. This makes you a kinder and more understanding friend for your horse. Feeling happy can improve your training with your horse and help you both enjoy spending time together.

Smiling also changes how you stand and move, making you look friendly and easy to approach. Horses can see these signals and often copy them, which creates a happy and peaceful atmosphere. This sharing of good feelings helps you and your horse feel closer and more connected.

Having a cheerful attitude can improve the whole environment. Staying positive and smiling often helps make the space around you more enjoyable and healthy for everyone, including your horse.

In short, smiling is a powerful and simple way to improve your time with horses. It helps create a good relationship, builds trust, and makes learning together easier. When you make smiling part of your time with horses, you build a bond based on understanding, respect, and shared happiness.

ABOUT THE AUTHOR

Marcel Olivé is a distinguished author, expert in Natural Horsemanship, and horse and hoof care specialist. With a deep passion for equine well-being, Marcel integrates horses into his practice as an Equine-Assisted Facilitator and Leadership and Performance Coach. His extensive knowledge and transformational approaches have made him a respected figure in the equestrian community, where he continues to inspire and educate through his writing and hands-on work with both horses and humans.

Printed in Great Britain
by Amazon